A Salve For Every Sore

A Salve for Every Sore

poems by

April Bulmer

Cormorant Books

Published with the assistance of the Canada Council and the Ontario Arts Council.

The author wishes to acknowledge the following magazines and periodicals where some of this material has or will appear: *Los, Passages,* and *The Malahat Review*. ACCESS Alberta broadcast early versions of “Angels”, “Indians”, “Tooth”, “Stump” and “Wild Rice”.

The characters in this work are fictional, and any resemblance to people living or dead is coincidental.

Cover from an oil on canvas, *Le Chapeau Espagnol*, by Jan Funnekotter, courtesy of the artist.

Printed and bound in Canada.

Published by Cormorant Books
RR 1
Dunvegan, Ontario
Canada K0C 1J0

Canadian Cataloguing in Publication Data

Bulmer, April, 1963-

A salve for every sore

ISBN 0-920953-66-2

I. Title.

PS8553.U49S24 1991 C811'.54 C91-090414-6
PR9199.3.B84S24 1991

For June and Helen

Acknowledgements

My thanks to the faculty and students in the Graduate Creative Writing program at Concordia University, in particular my thesis advisor, Professor Henry Beissel.

I was most fortunate to spend the Spring of 1989 at the Banff Centre for the Arts; thank you to Don Coles, Don McKay, Adele Wiseman, P.K. Page, Miriam Waddington, and Joyce Marshall for their editorial advice.

I am grateful to my friends Karen Massey, David McGimpsey, and Andrea Ivan for their support and guidance.

Thanks to "Dad-Only" for his ways.

TABLE OF CONTENTS

I Will Keep My Mouth With a Bridle

All Thy Garments Smell of Myrrh

My Heart Was Hot Within Me

Praise Him with the Timbrel and Dance

Incline thine ear unto my cry.

Psalm 88:2

Indians

They're in the orchard again.
Dark bodies stretch between limbs and shadows.
Hands grasp for the hard fruit.
A few pull their red lips around the apples.
The white flesh glistens on their teeth like spit.

They have come in trucks and narrow boats.

Father and I load up the Chevy behind the store:
tobacco, canned goods, vanilla extract,
vegetables, fruit, chocolate.

At the camp some of the women are standing
in the hungry mouths of tepees. (Hunger everywhere:
in the growling of dogs and wet cries
of shoeless children. Even the lake is empty.)

Father trades tins for silver coins.

One of the women smiles at me, she is chewing the end
of a ragged braid. Her belly is swollen and her breasts
are big and round like the melons we brought to sell.

I pass her a bag of oranges when Father is busy.
She motions me close and unfastens
the pink-pebbled necklace she wears
like a second smile. She drapes it round my pale neck.
It breaks my surface like a handful of little stones.

Stump

Elmer Sidney wanders the baked-goods aisle,
his stump thrust into a long leather change-purse,
pecking like the bag is full of seeds.

His hand was once a wild bird
caught in his own threshing machine.
Fingers flew like pink feathers.

In his dream the cut wrist gasps
like a largemouth bass.

In his dream the hand sprouts
from his turnip patch.
It swells like a breast,
a slender piglet sucks
each moist fingertip.

Elmer is thumping on the front counter.
I see it out of the pouch,
a footless ankle wearing a big green sock.

A limp puppet waving me to the cash.

Dulcie

They all stunk like Billy-be-damned when I first met them. But the little girl, Dulcie, was pretty, her hair long and yellow as corn. Father talked about them at dinner, how they'd been eating pig mash mixed with a bit of molasses for six weeks, and how he'd given them some bully beef and a few cans of beans on credit. Mrs Webster wears the same shabby dress every time she comes into the store, but Mother says she's nice.

Dulcie told us about the grasshoppers. It was worse than in the Bible, she said. They travelled in a cloud that darkened the sun like an eclipse and she and her brother watched them through broken pieces of green glass they held to their eyes like specs. Those locusts could eat a broom, even the handle, all they'd leave would be the metal band that kept the bristles together and it would lie in the dirt like when Dulcie's big sister lost her wedding ring. And the 'hoppers (that's what she calls them) spit brown juice like Elmer Sidney when he chews tobacco. And once her brother threw a leather glove against the side of the barn and it stuck. Mr Webster told Father they ate the halters off his team and the seat of his John Deere tractor.

Danny Webster told my sister one of their horses got the bloat and they shot it. Then they walked away, left all their farm equipment—big machines that kind of looked like animal carcasses in the desert. Mrs Webster told Mother the wind blows all the time. It's like a deep breath from the land's great swollen lungs. She could never get her laundry white. *The curtains, the sheets, the little feller's diapers—grey as the sky. The prairie's a dusty floor to the Lord. And God's sweeping Saskatchewan clean.*

They prayed Christ might appear as a bearded man with sore feet and an empty belly, or as a winged angel who could crack the horizon's spine, smooth the prairie with His white palm as if it were the page of a big book.

Onion

Balanced on Eliza Jane Davidson's palm, a perfect Christmas ball. Her fingernails are lined in black like a fancy lady's eyes. There is mud on the face of her old wrist watch. She hooks the stem around her green thumb, wraps it in the soft pleats of a cabbage. A slug clings to her sleeve—dull cuff-link.

Father gives her $1.90 for the bushel of vegetables. Eliza Jane Davidson buys a pull of tobacco and a box of yellow tulip bulbs. Rolls a cigarette on the counter, blows lines of smoke, angel-hair fine.

Fiddler

Charlie Davidson's big shoe taps time.
He's out front leaning against a worn mattress.
Strokes his fiddle's long locks,
makes her cry as if untangling knots.

Charlie's mongrel chews an old bone,
grass-stained as a horse's hoof.

Eliza Jane weeds her potato patch.
The tubers are curls
on the earth's dark belly.

Shack's on fire.
The roof is a woman's wide hat
and beneath it she shakes
her flaming red mane. The windows
are sad bloodshot eyes.

I am delivering two bags of groceries,
hold them like they are nursing babies.
My mouth is open, I want to lick
the air's dry lips.

I leave the brown paper bags, orphans
in a patch of wild rhubarb.

I am running from this scene:
the half-witted fiddler,
the inbred dog,

the woman who loves
the mongoloid faces of potatoes,
their bald heads.

I run from the broken brim,
the burning hair,
the blistered scalp.

Eddy Goss

He buys a blue salt block and a big bag of oyster shells for his chickens. Tells me:

> Jesus Loving Christ, she makes a
> man feel lowly, with her beauty
> and never takin a lover. I was
> drinkin a bottle a Orange Kik
> when I seen her cross the field
> in her summer work dress, her
> boots round her neck so's she
> wouldn't wear them out. I heard
> her singin *Little Betty Blue*
> *lost her holiday shoe,* as
> she got close. She had a apple
> box a rags and dirty clothes. I
> watched her dark head bend over
> the water like she was a whisperin
> her sins to the rocks.
>
> Sure would like to take tea and
> porridge cakes with Miss Graham.
> To rub the soreness from her body
> at the end of the day with
> a bit a fish oil.
>
> I'm saving my treaures so her
> Pa'll let me have her. I got a
> sack a onions, two jars a pickled
> eggs, a piece a lace curtain, a
> ostrich-feathered hat, two skinny

cows, and a sorry-lookin scrub
horse. Give all I got to spoon
with Miss Laura Graham. To share
with her my daily bread, a
glimpse of the moon.

Rose

Rose Beasley is a worn-out woman. She stands in front of our store, a basket of violets and daisies over her thin arm. Once she also tried to sell her gravy-boat and a few crummy oil paintings, and Father asked her what the Sam Hill was going on.

She knows all that lives is holy, so tries to give her kids good things, though the youngest got the black tongue. Every morning, she stirs a huge open kettle of oatmeal for her children, dumps in peas and beans and handfuls of raisins. Stirs that big heaving mass with a stick. Sometimes for dinner, she serves cow's heart stuffed with breadcrumbs.

She wears a saint's medallion at her neck. When she hasn't sold a posy, I see her lips move and her hand trace the sign of the cross over her dirty blouse. Told me once she says three Hail Mary's and throws her rosary over the clothes-line when her flowers aren't budding and she needs sunshine.

Angels

I measure George Sidney's shoulders
for a belladonna back plaster. *The pain feels*
like broken wings, he says.

He tells me the angels came again last night
as he was brewing tea.
Appeared as steam on the kitchen window,
rustled in the gingham curtains.
Five of them stretched
from the oven to the icebox,
clean and white as nighties drying on the line.
Then they fluttered like moths
around the light bulb.
George flaps his arms and gives an arthritic wince.
And sang, sang hymns as the kettle whistled.
George makes a soprano squawk.

They beat their feathered arms, rose
like prayers through the stained ceiling.

Winnie

She is an Ojibway girl from across the lake. I like the stories she tells of the great thunderbirds who nest in the rocks and of her grandfather, a medicine man, who knows the secrets of frog and turtle. Once he cured her of pneumonia by sucking the sickness from her lungs with a hollow bear-bone. And when she was well she tied a plug of tobacco with ribbons and a claw, left it by the water in the bear's honour.

Winnie tells me she has felt Spirit in the muzzle of a Jersey cow, and in a cold bottle of buttermilk. And once when she was mending her fish nets she could feel her fingers untangling a shape, and knew that Spirit was there in that loose weave.

Winnie teaches me an Indian game played with wild plumstones. We toss them out back behind Father's store. When it is my turn, Winnie makes steeples with her big brown hands, crooked spires.

Then she drags her feet back to the reserve through mud, burr, and bramble. Sings to the rhythm of muscle and breath.

At night I hear the wind rub its nose in the dirt and think of Winnie sleeping beside her mama in their birch-bark tent. Spirit sniffing out their scent, then lying down outside the flap like a dog.

What profit is there in my blood, when I go down to the pit?
Shall the dust praise thee?

Psalm 30: 9

Clarence

Last night, Clarence on the plum wine. Even the moon gagged from its white sack. A faint stink on the lake's thin skin. Clarence's palms, his shirt sleeves anointed with lake water and mud. Barking frogs died in his fist—beaded evening bags.

This morning, clutching the waistband of his trousers, he blows his nose into his hand, throws the snot into the reeds. It hangs like plant spittle.

Margaret shares his packed lunch. Clarence tells my sister he got his boots stuck in the Depression gumbo-mud and never pulled loose. Doesn't even have a pair of boots now, wears woollen socks and a couple of burlap bags stuffed inside rubbers.

Once he was out back when I went to hang laundry on the line. Told me he used to work at the Distinctive Handle Co. *Painted broom handles by dipping them into a pipe a paint, knew how to work with two colours to make em real pretty.*

Had a wife named Lacy and a little baby he called Nanna cause she looked like his grandma when she was born with that kinky red hair a hers. He used to like to come home to his Lacy and their daughter always clean and in white diapers. Sometimes she'd have a rash from the heat and he would tend to her with toilet waters and creams. He liked it there in their blue clapboard house on the prairie. He liked it that they had tea bags and fancy cups with saucers. Liked watching his wife sew pink curtains. Still remembers her tea-rose scent when he pressed his lips to her white neck. Remembers her beating his work shirts and her print shifts on the rocks by the river. The little cries she'd make when she had her lady's problems, how he'd rub her tummy swollen beneath the cotton night-gown. Remembers.

28 When he lost his job painting brooms, he scrubbed their wood floors, massaged Lacy's red feet at night. Sang to Nanna, songs that made him sniff and dab at his eyes. Saw despair in Lacy's fleshy arm as she stirred pots of gopher stew. Disdain from the porch—him dragging home a catch of trapped coyotes.

One day—the crocheted table cloth, the good blue china, his girls—gone. All night he rocked in an old wooden chair, sang songs that made him sniff and dab at his eyes.

Clarence rode the rods from the west, thinking up poems for Lacy and Nanna. Hung like a bat from the underbelly of the train.

Spotted Calf

I am folding flannel shirts when Leighton McCallister plants himself on an apple crate. Tells me:

> Ya know, Marie, had this truck, painted
> her yellow. Headed west with an
> Indian girl I found in the hills. She
> had some blankets, some clothes, a
> skinnin knife. Pretty lookin gal. And
> I'd heard Indian women don't cry as much.
>
> She always got a stew pot goin
> so we was never hungry. And we was
> cosy as cooties, snuggled up in my
> tent at night.
>
> One day, me and Spotted Calf met a
> feller when we was camped outside a
> Regina, they used to call it Pile a
> Bones, ya know that? Anyways this
> feller wanted to strike a bit of a deal.
> He says, *give ya a suckin pig for that*
> *cheap coat a yours, or how bout some*
> *candles for a spoon and them wool*
> *socks*. Well, we didn't need nothin he
> had to offer. So finally he says, he
> says to me, *give ya ten bucks for that*
> *there squaw*. And ya know, Marie, I
> was runnin kinda low on gas, and ten
> bucks was clover, rain in the desert.
> So I heaved all her stuff out of the
> truck and took the money. But ya know
> it's not true what I heard about
> Indian gals, cause her cheeks was all
> wet when I drove off.

Walter

A pale Indian screamed into the tree's throat.
Leaves were bloody tongues licking his wound
and the chainsaw's grinding teeth.

A hammock of nerves and tendons stretched
between knee and calf, a loose weave that gave.
Walter's leg fell between branches, a dead limb.
The chain saw thrashed in the dirt,
a red smear on the blade, a gasping gill.

Now Walter's face is a swollen apple bobbing
in front of the store. The short leg straddles
our tree, his plaid arms fit the blade
into its split sex, it falls open like a woman.

Walter's crutch pocks the dirt. The new stump is
a tough calf beneath the rolled pant leg.

Shoes

When our shoes become snug
Father removes their tips.
Slices their tongues
to silence our feet.

At school my toes
are white teeth in angry mouths.
They growl at Jane Tilly's
patent leathers (black-lipped
jaws of smug dogs.)

Buckles

School house, two miles from home.
A hill in the last stretch, green,
steep as the back of a dragon.

I one-two-three step.
A swish of the great tail
could send me into the marsh
where snakes lie like fallen necklaces,
beetles are black sequins,
and the mud opens its moist mouth
to swallow young girls.
It sucks their fine ankles,
spits shoe buckles
into the tall grass
like bones.

Teacher

Miss McBroom twitches
on the floor among cloakroom clothes.

Her eyes roll like blue marbles,
her body tosses on a bed
of duffel coats and woollen scarves.

I lay my thick red pencil
across her eraser-pink tongue.
My fingers are quivering pieces
of chalk moist with her spit.

The school bell rings;
she comes round rubbing
a red mitten against her cheek.

Class Photograph

Margaret is in the front row, a pale
child hugging her belly. Her head strains
towards Eugene Hamstead's ear, a dirty shell.
And look—between overall cuff and boot,
the bully's ankle, fine as a wrist.

I stand beside Miss McBroom, my arm brushes her
monogrammed sweater. I feel the swell of her
bosom, $3.00 foundation wired and sensible;
imagine her holding Mr Buttersworth
against those firm beige cups.

Spring Assembly

I'm singing
Alice Blue Gown
solo at the spring assembly.
Margaret is at the organ.

My chiffon dress blows
like a sheer curtain.
Something is caught
inside the fine gauze and fluttering.
It is my heart.

My fingers clasp round each other—
talons on a branch.
My high notes fly
from a small cage,
flap through hair.
Fold their wings,
nest in safe hollows.

Beasts, and all cattle; creeping things, and flying fowl.

Psalm 148: 10

Brother

Sweet cob of corn
husked in Mama's arms.

Spittle on her nipple,
fresh nightgown folded
at her feet. I cradle
an armful of wet lilac
and apple blossom. A fallen

petal is a birthmark
on my brother's forehead.

Feeding

Mother holds Victor's hungry mouth
against her open shift. Her knees
are swollen like preserved peaches.

The kitchen floor is scrubbed.
I play in the corner,
wrap my doll in a flannel diaper.

Victor burps. A line of blue milk
runs down Mother's breast like a vein.
Margaret kneels before Mother and Child:
marble Mary, stony Saviour.

She feeds Mother's kneecaps
thick white cream from a glass jar,
moisturizes the pale swell of flesh.

Now I am crayoning a brown paper bag,
purpling fat circles,
perfect plums. Can taste
the sweet spit juicing
from their gums.

Cow

Lowing, rocking
a warm heart in a cradle.
Swinging the loose folds of flesh
that blanket her unborn calf.

Her hide is a bunting bag.

I'm pulling at her teats,
tugging at a beast's mother.

Moo Moo   the idiot syllables,
Moo Moo   a blue lullaby.

Her tail is swift
as a fiddling bow,
she's shooing flies.

Victor's making music with teaspoons,
now he's catching the milk
in one of their silver bellies.
Quiver quiver
before he takes it on his tongue.

Tin pail, barnyard stink,
tickle in my scalp, wet sleeve.

The moon is a clean kitchen plate,
the morning a pink table cloth.

The cat sleeps in the manger,
the cow chews long blonde hay.

She swallows, opens her great mumbling lips.
Moo Moo   the sweet cattle myth.

Chicken

Heart and gizzard,
for Chum. Wet pouch
for a wagging tail.

Mother cradles it in the sink,
washes blemished skin
with a moist blue rag.
Salts wounds, plucks
a few coarse hairs.

I break bread
into the red bowl, shake
sage over the torn white flesh,
grass-stained manna.

Mother sings
of all clean birds ye shall eat.

Victor sucks an oven mitt.
His fist is balled inside.
Bakers' men . . . mark it with V.

I squeeze the dressing into
shapes: a collapsed lung, swollen
kidney, pale spleen.

My hand is gloved
inside the fowl's empty casing,
a dark cavity like me.

I will keep my mouth with a bridle.

Psalm 39: 1

Dummy

Mrs Hamstead tells Father that Dummy died in his mother's arms. She was feeding her forty-three-year-old son with a teaspoon when he clucked as if to utter his first word, a word like a rough stone his voice had never polished. But it was a gasp he swallowed, his last breath.

After the stroke, Dummy lay in bed for seven months holding a rag to a slim stream of saliva. His tongue flapped like the loose sole of a boot.

Even before the illness they said he had rocks in his head, but I know it was the strand of precious words he dreamed of stringing. They were not the words he scribbled to me on scratch pads—eggs, flour, milk—pale names their owners wore like cardigans. They were blue and green and orange, big beaded words that would have made a woman beautiful had he been able to offer them to her.

Mother sends Ruthie to the door with a fistful of pansies when we hear Dummy has passed on. Dummy, a quiet blond man who liked lemonade and Sweet Marie bars.

Soup

Mother boils bones till
they're smooth as knuckles. Tempts
the pot's dark mouth with vegetables.

She wipes the hot breath
from her wrist like a dog's wet kiss.

Mother's wooden spoon is
a slow tongue. She offers
her soup fine onion-clippings,
slim-fingered carrots,
potato slivers like broken teeth.

After school I filled my lunch box
with wild watercress. Now I toss
handfuls into the broth. They seem
to sprout from the marrow
like the hairs from Father's fist.

Ruthie

Mother's cheek is a broken
bird, handful of flesh and bones.
Later, her hand is a damp fish,
caught in a door's quick beak.

My sister, still a tadpole,
beats beneath her water.

Crows

At dawn I sweep the dirt
and haul baskets of pumpkins and gourds.

Across the lake, a crow circles—
a wild cinder caught
in a puff of factory smoke.

It is cold. My heart knows
the hardness of turnip.

Last week, I helped a farmer
harvest armfuls of sooty cabbage
and black stumps. They were hauled
away in wheelbarrows, then burned.

I listened for the wind's death hymn,
heard only the lament of crows.

Cousin Cora

The cutlery claps in the drawers.
The smooth palms of spoons applaud
till they bend backwards.

Cousin Cora curtsies to the blank-faced
cupboards, now she's zipping up
her majorette boots, fastening
the strap of a tall blue hat.

She marches around Victor's
high chair, pumping her arms.
Her baton circles
above appliances, hits
the oven and falls from
its white cheek, like a dull knife.

Laundry Room

I am thin and pale
as a dress pattern. My lips
are a hem, stitched and ironed.

Mother's swollen hands
peg laundry to the line.
Her black brassiere
quivers like a bat.
Victor's brown stocking cap
is a wet rat suspended
from the tail.

Pickled beets press
noses to glass.
The cat paws the jar—
smash. Mother drops
Victor's socks, they
stub their soft toes.

The beets' heads break open
like boils. She scoops their flesh
into a wash bucket, the blood
stains her stiff cuffs.

Hallowe'en

I am a bride, wear a veil fine as Queen Anne's Lace.
Soon—pressed violets, clean linen, tarnished
silver, the old iron bed. Crumpets, a chest of
drawers, custard pie.

My gown drags in the dirt. Margaret, Ruthie,
and Victor have run-ahead—three
buckskinned Indians humming in the snake
language. My brother beats on a child's tom-
tom.

We are in the hills behind the store when I
tear a hole in my bag of treats, leave a
sweet trail for the bridegroom.

Eliza Jane Davidson tosses a wormy apple into
each of our pillow cases. A hillbilly stink in
the old kitchen, a candle burning in a
hollowed-out potato. Charlie plays his fiddle.
The old blue tune smells like wild-rose blooms,
a bride's reel.

Percy Starr wears a dark narrow suit, bows
and claps his gloved hands as we enter the
lobby of his broken hotel. He has sewn
little sacks with needle and thread, stuffed
them with sour drops. He takes my lacy hand,
kisses the red stone of my engagement ring.
His oiled hair brushes my face.

I run, follow Victor's rhythm, my sisters' chants, braids, and coloured ribbons. They are at the edge of the orchard when I see a haunt, a round woman rising from the marsh gas. I throw her my bouquet, the flowers quiver in her white hands. I can hear her breath, and the slow stroke of her lover's paddle. I hear a rustle of crinoline as the slim boat takes her to shore.

Blades

Snow fine as face powder
on the frozen lake.

Ruthie plays on the shore,
tugs at the weeds
sprouting from the ice
like wild hairs
from an old woman's cheek.

Margaret and I wear
the brown hockey-skates
Father bought second-hand
for a dollar.

Our silver blades cut
the taut skin, leave
slim scars.

Tooth

Margaret crosses the highway behind Father.
He reaches the mailbox and fingers
its mumpish cheek.

Father is reading the telephone bill
when he hears her whine. The traffic
is a great coloured rope weaving
around my frightened sister.

A brown pick-up wears a streak
of her blood like war paint.

Father carries the awkward package,
a delivery he never ordered.

Mother is washing the linoleum floor
when he unwraps their daughter. Father wipes
away the blood and big tears that cling
to the fruit-patterned oilcloth on the table.

I cut dresses from the Eaton's Catalogue
paste them on a cardboard girl.

Outside, my sister's tooth is slowly sinking
into the pavement's soft shoulder.

My parents have left Margaret
on a hard kitchen chair.
Her smile is a broken comb
and she is crying into the curly blue arms
of her own cardigan.

All thy garments smell of myrrh, and aloes, and cassia.

Psalm 45: 8

Quack

A salve fer every sore, gerls.
Bud digs his pinkie into a white jar
as into an itchy ear.
He rubs the yellow wax
into my wrist—a pale circle
like after I wear my watch in the sun.

Gray's Balm, balm a Gilead
reliable antiseptic an healer
for relief a mumps, whooooping cough,
nasal catarrh, boils, chilblains, piles, hayfeva,
rheumatic pains, mosquita bites.

Had ta take cancer off the label
but it ain't bad for that neither.

He coughs, points to a row of warts
at the cuff of Ruthie's red dress.
Doctor up those unsightlies
wit a bit a balm
and a scrap a flannel,
fall off like buttons.

I apply it to Margaret's blue lip
and the scab on her chin—
thick cream into pie crust.

A dime for a little drum of miracle lard.
Bud stares at the coin on his palm,

a blister to be anointed.
Big fambly—yous' ll need more than a jar
an your pa' ll want
couple a cases for the store.
I shake my head.
Guess poverdy is the motha a health.

Loads his swollen bag into the trunk
of his blue boneshaker, boneshakes away.

Hips

Mother breaks eggs, stirs
a clot of yellow milk.

At the butcher block Father pounds
until the loins are tender.
Now they fry face down,
move their hips, whine.

I heal the blemished skin of plates,
see my own face in the dish-water:
Marie, a thin child, frill
of soap suds at her neck.

I want to be big of breast
like Eleanor Klintworth. I
want to know blood and tea
and the secrets of monthlies.

I wipe my image with the wash-rag,
it swells and quivers.

Bicycle

I balance on Rollie Hubbard's
handle bars. Miss McBroom sent
me home. Fever rides my bones,
my stomach bucks. Rollie says
it's the Double Evecheka*
giving me collywobbles.

Rollie's a half-breed, lives at the lake's
rough elbow. His mama's a Midewiwin**,
knows her roots. Father buys her sweet teas,
the little sacks she stuffs with rose hips,
licorice fern, wild ginger.

Sometimes Rollie delivers rough
baskets of Indian breadroot, wapato tubers,
nettle shoots, plums.

The bicycle rounds the lake's nape.
Our tires massage the road's dark skin.

I spit up in Mother's flower bed.
Chum sniffs and wags. Rollie cleans
the chain's dirty teeth.

* A child's term for flu.

** Member of secret Ojibway society which uses herbs and roots for medicinal purposes.

Mary Strawberry

Rollie's mama bathes her cousin in a wash bucket behind
their shack. The sores on her back weep. Mrs. Hubbard dabs
them with a cool cloth and sweet-smelling leaf.

Mary Strawberry's heart is a deer-hide bag. The charms—
secrets of bug, herb and root—lost to the heel
of her husband's boot, a dog's sniff.

Mrs. Hubbard trims Mary's dark mane. The black hair lies
damp in the dirt like a killed squirrel.

Blessed Virgin took Mary Strawberry's daughter
in the moons of her youth. Smell of mice and angels
when the Black Robes carried her out.

Mary Strawberry ate ketchup sandwiches for supper.
Then gave a long sad chant at the bosom
of the water. Clutched a root-sewn basket of
rosaries, beaver bones, a bear's front teeth.

Mr Beauchamp

He is very sad, though Mrs Hubbard has brought him a medicine egg coloured light blue. Mr Beauchamp's wife, Lily, died last night between their flannel sheets. Mr Beauchamp shaved and boiled water before he noticed Lily, white and stiff beneath her rayon night-gown.

Friends gather in the parlour to drink the widower's tea. Mrs Hubbard plays the drums of sorrow while Mr Beauchamp gathers Lily's belongings: hand mirror, pile of hairpins, girdle, hot-water bottle, feather mop, handful of loose buttons, seven pressed tea towels, an unanswered chain letter. Mrs Hubbard says death has cabbaged Lily and she will want these where she is going. She has brought her a bowl of wild rice and blueberries, some jerkied meat, pickled fish in jars. And amulets, bones, and feathers in a soft medicine bag.

Get out her rubber boots and a blanket, Mrs Hubbard tells Mr Beauchamp. *There's a son of a bitchin wind blowin and she got rivers to wade.*

Stinks, Potions, and Medications:

If your muscles ache or you want to ripen a few boils, sandwich your poultice with mashed potatoes, oatmeal, or mush.

You can also use the lining of eggshells to bring your boil or carbuncle to a head.

Bandage your chest with a few cooked onions to loosen up a tight cold.

If your kid has the croup, burn a rag and wrap the scorched cloth round his neck.

If you need to take a pee, but can't, brew up some watermelon tea.

Soak a bit of cotton with lemon and pack it round your gums if you have a bad tooth.

Brew up a pot of pumpkin tea so as to dry up a nasty tape-worm.

Sulphur blown into your throat through a bird's quill will relieve you of the sore.

A bit of mutton tallow on your cracked knuckles in winter makes them soft as a babe's.

Measle suffering is relieved with a dose of sheep-pellet tea.

If you have bad insect bites, put a cud of tobacco on the
 sting.

If your nose is bleeding, chew a wad of paper.

If you're a lady with the bed menses, take some tansy tea.

If you've got a bad burn, scrape a bit of tuber flesh on it.

Child Birthing:

If you're expecting, and you've got a big mouth, you'll have an easy birthing.

Hold a short metal chain and key over the mother's belly. If it turns in circles, it'll be a girl. It'll move back and forth for a boy.

If you're going to be a mother, and you want a boy, eat a lot of peanuts. Eat sweets should you want a girl.

Keep all your house doors open and take out all your bottle stoppers if you want an easy birthing.

After the babe is born, rub it with lard and spit on it, so it'll be happy.

Apply a liberal portion of horse manure to a freshly severed cord.

Don't cut your babe's finger or toe nails for a year, for it's sure to fall ill.

If your babe's got the mouth fungus, find a man whose never seen his pap to breathe into it.

Wet nursing is best if you're a woman whose maiden and married name are the same.

If your babe's whining, make a sugar tit. Tie a few cubes in a thin cloth and let it suck.

Don't wash your kid's right hand should you want it to be wealthy.

Babes should always be weaned on Good Friday unless the trees are in bloom.

Wash your babe's knees in dishwater to make it walk sooner.

If your babe's teething, let it chew a bit of the skin from your cured pork.

Keep your babe from mirrors for the first four months, so as to prevent rickets.

GOD BLESS ALL YOUR BLOOD, FLESH, MARROW, AND BONES.

Prayer

In the root cellar.
My kneecaps are the dirty skins
potatoes wear.
I bear the yoke,
I am the young woman who
weepeth sore in the night, putteth
her face to the dust.

O Lord, open my lips
and my mouth
shall show forth
thy praise.

My heart was hot within me, while I was musing the fire burned: then spake I with my tongue.

Psalm 39: 3

Dandelion Wine

Dandelions: sticky fur,
wild cats sunning
on the grass. My fingers
comb their yellow manes,
clip their tails.

Water and a teaspoon of sugar
tame them. I hide
the bottles in a dark den.

August evening:
Ruthie, Margaret and I sip
from Mother's Sunday glasses.
Borrowed beads, moist lips
the tip of a fancy hanky.

The wine is clear as urine.
It bites our tongues.
We are wild as weeds.

Wild Rice

Johnny's boat parts the green reeds, he
flails them into the canoe.
Grain scatters like beads.

The men twist among cattails
and watercress, their dangerous bodies
stir the thick marsh. Brown hands
quick as fish mouths spit
rice into the boat.

On the shore they feed it into sacks,
load up the truck's flat belly.

Johnny drives her hard, steers
with a firm grip, rubs
his worn cord-breeches.
Her wide hips rock.

At the store he pulls the key
from the ignition. She jerks.
He grabs each burlap neck,
heaves bags like he's drowning pups.

I take a bundle in my arms;
a wet shifting beneath the rough skin.

Christmas

Victor and Ruthie hang red balls on the tree.
Margaret lights candles. We sing of angels
and mild mercy.

Outside on the frozen lake the Indians fish
by spear and torch. They squat over holes
under blankets and tiny wigwams.
Their soft boots make prints in the snow.

This is Christmas—a blood stain, a crooked knife,
a gasp, a man's steady hands. A bag of wet life
pulled silently by sled.

Later, a lamp in the dark, the shadows of women—
their wide hips, their loose red shawls.

Christmas, a ceremony, a simple grace:
steady chant, burn of sweet-smelling herbs.
Lore of scale, bone, flesh, and bladder.

Woman

I am the grocer's daughter,
a country cousin
with a poor haircut.

I am a weak little woman
who menstruates now,
who hides soft white pads
among her hankies and undershirts.

Monthly I ache,
have a cry.
Monthly I wear a pink belt and pins.

I am a pale lady
making my way to school
carrying a jelly sandwich,
a thermos of milk,
and a green apple
in a tin lunch box.

The boys pass me on bicycles
ringing their bells.
The girls run by
swinging book bags.

I am wearing rubber galoshes
and a red tassel cap.
My purple leotards and pleated skirt
hide the iodine-stained gauze.

I am bandaged and bruised.
I nurse a new hurt.

Praise him with the timbrel and dance: praise him with stringed instruments and organs.

Psalm 150: 4

Trapeze

Rollie Hubbard is no circus lad.
He has never ridden bare-back,
never smelled a lion's hot breath.

He juggled oranges for that girl,
embroidered darkness with gypsy song.
He does not know she can grind
an organ better than a monkey, squeeze
love from an accordion.

He shuffles his hobnail boots, she sways
her turquoise hips, pushes her rhinestones
into his stiff dungarees.

He fancies himself Houdini tonight, but
too many bouquets blossom from his
sleeves, rabbits breed in his socks. And she
untwists him like a magician's hanky.
He doesn't know men train for such feats.
She loosens the knots that bind
each coloured scarf. He has never felt
red, purple, blue . . .

Love Prescription

I have come to Mrs Hubbard for a love-magic prescription. Her son, Rollie, is at the sweetheart dance with the circus lady, mooning and smooching and swooning around her in his no. 13 boots. I am plum sad.

Mrs Hubbard says I have come to the right hospital. Rollie has swallowed a dose of Will Strawberry's bad medicine. She smelled it on the lake's breath.

She had braids of sweetgrass, a stew kettle of grubs and hoppers, rabbit root and balsam, fresh weeds that have raised a cream. Mrs Hubbard is a good healer.

She snips a hank of my hair, tamps it inside the moist head of a sparrow. Scrapes the white dust from the dried belly of a frog; makes a sound like she's buttering toast. She stuffs the head inside a small hide bag. I tuck it beneath the ribbon strap of my bandeau, close to my bust. I'll wear it till next blood stain, or till I smell lust.

Juggler

I finger-waved my hair
rubbed up my pumps with a rag.
Rollie sighs, *ain't ya a*
gasper, a beauty.

We reel around the Babe Ruth
clutch-an'-hug dancing.
He tells me a poem about a juggler:
Oh, he balances a broom on his nose,
tosses kitchen plates into the air.

Oh, Oh, I have three hearts
and Rollie's set them on fire. Catches
them in one hand and kisses me.

Tattoo

Rollie writes me letters from the Ojibway reserve where he spends summer. Tells me he collects animal bones and pink stones from fields. Tells me he tripped carrying a lardpail of breadmush and took six stitches in the head.

Then a postcard from Toronto, a red streetcar pulling itself along a track:

> Rode to the city in the back of my brother's
> pickup with the dog who liked the way the wind
> combed his big coat. Drank a beer and watched
> some girls twist their hips in dark corners.
> My tattoo scabbed like a bad knee, wore
> a square of gauze for a week. Could have
> had a picture of a sailing ship or a naked
> lady, but I got an eagle cause if you can
> catch an eagle feather you're a man before
> it touches the earth.

I practice dancing in my fancies when it's night, swaying like a Toronto gal. Imagine the taste of blue wings, the curve of beak and talon.

Dear Rollie,

I am in the orchard, have picked us both an apple. Yours I shined in the hem of my skirt.

Father has built a snack bar at the side of the store. I serve hot dogs and milk whips to Toronto girls and their beaus. It is so hot and my customers smell of tanning oil and Noxzema. I am still pale.

I have been cutting hair in my bedroom at night. I set a towel, a rat-tail comb, and a glass dish of pink wave-set on my vanity. I must say it is rather professional. Last week, I gave Rose Beasley a marcelle, and Mrs. Benson has made an appointment for a trim on Friday. I have saved enough money to buy more supplies and have ordered Madame X Aids to a Lovely Coiffure: water-wave combs, roll-n-pin end curlers, and vassar wavers for long bobs.

If you were here, I would sneak you a chocolate broom and a square of sponge toffee from the store. If you were here, I would cut your dark hair handsome-like.

I miss you, Rollie. I miss your fiddling music, how it hung among the fruit trees. I miss that honey tin you carried on our walks and filled with the arrow heads and sharpened stones we found in fields.

Have you learned your people's names for grasses and secret flowers? Will you teach me the Ojibway for violet, maiden hair, and Indian paintbrush?

Do you remember my scent and the pulse you felt under my cuddle-puff bolero?

I will meet your train in new shoes and a Hollywood halo hat (as worn by Loretta Young).

Love, Your Marie XOX

Indian, Lover

Indian, Soldier, Lover, Cowboy
all summer you ran wild
with your people. Sucked
Grape Island's dark sweet
nipples. Stroked your oar
as if it were a woman's thigh.

I bought cuban heels.

Now I sit by the tracks.
The wind is nervous.
The weeds give a good smell here.

The cows wait for your train
as I do. Our white faces:
full moons.

Breath

Sleep is an angel cradling Rollie. I hold him in my arms and feel her breath against my cheek. She has hung her wings on a branch in the willow. She loves my half-breed, presses her lips to his tattoo, fingers the belongings he has bound with two leather thongs—flannel shirt, fiddle, three pink stones, can of tobacco, palm-sized Bible. She likes the knife he found in the dirt, half the blade gone, *that's a good thing,* she tells him.

She ties a long cord round his trousers and drags him like an idiot. She teaches him how to bleed a white geranium red, how to remove a coyote's heart and stitch it into a weak child's chest. She licks a flat stone, presses her thumb into its belly and peels back the skin. She shows him the fat muscle white as a fist punching the air.

Chicken Fest

I won't be my father's Jack
I won't be my mother's Jill
I will be the fiddler's wife
And have music when I will.

Rollie Hubbard's waxy ear
holds the future. A gypsy moth
beats from his flannel sleeve to rest
on the palm of a spoon.

The fiddle and his bow lie
like newly-wed lovers:
his thin arm across her broad hips.

Rollie and I pass words like a pipe. Take
them between our teeth and swallow.

I kiss a wine bottle's green lips and eat
moon-ginger pie with a twisted fork.

In the parlour my fella makes
fiddling music. I dance the buck and wing,
then two-step with a broom handle,
blue shoes flying like a bride's bouquet.